SCOTT FORESMAN

READING STREET

KINDERGARTEN

COMMON CORE ©

Program Authors

Peter Afflerbach

Camille Blachowicz

Candy Dawson Boyd

Elena Izquierdo

Connie Juel

Edward Kame'enui

Donald Leu

Jeanne R. Paratore

P. David Pearson

Sam Sebesta

Deborah Simmons

Susan Watts Taffe

Alfred Tatum

Sharon Vaughn

Karen Kring Wixson

Glenview, Illinois

Boston, Massachusetts

Chandler, Arizona

Upper Saddle River, New Jersey

ALWAYS LEARNING

PEARSON

We dedicate Reading Street to
Peter Jovanovich.

His wisdom, courage,
and passion for education
are an inspiration to us all.

Accelerated Reader®

Acknowledgments appear on page 144, which constitutes an extension of this copyright page.

Copyright © 2013 Pearson Education, Inc., or its affiliates. All Rights Reserved. Printed in the United States of America. This publication is protected by copyright, and permission should be obtained from the publisher prior to any prohibited reproduction, storage in a retrieval system, or transmission in any form or by any means, electronic, mechanical, photocopying, recording, or likewise. For information regarding permissions, write to Rights Management & Contracts, Pearson Education, Inc., One Lake Street, Upper Saddle River, New Jersey 07458.

Pearson, Scott Foresman, and Pearson Scott Foresman are trademarks, in the U.S. and/or other countries, of Pearson Education, Inc., or its affiliates.

Common Core State Standards: © Copyright 2010. National Governors Association Center for Best Practices and Council of Chief State School Officers. All rights reserved.

PEARSON

ISBN-13: 978-0-328-72439-0
ISBN-10:   0-328-72439-4
4 5 6 7 8 9 10 V011 16 15 14 13 12

Dear Reader,

Now that you know about traveling down Reading Street, how would you like to meet George Washington? Do you know who George Washington is? If not, you'll soon find out. You're in for a treat.

George Washington, Little Panda, and other characters are all waiting to meet you.

As always, you'll need to bring along all your special skills for reading, writing, and thinking.

Buckle up, and let's get started.

Sincerely,
The Authors

Changes All Around Us

How do changes affect us?

Big Book

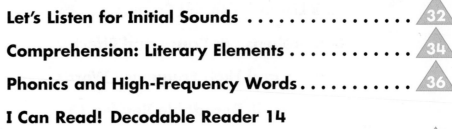

Week 2

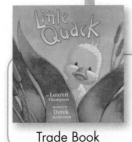

Trade Book

Unit 3 Contents

Week 5

Week 6

Don Leu
The Internet Guy

Right before our eyes, the nature of reading and learning is changing. The Internet and other technologies create new opportunities, new solutions, and new literacies. New reading comprehension skills are required online. They are increasingly important to our students and our society.

Those of us on the Reading Street team are here to help you on this new, and very exciting, journey.

See It!

- Big Question Video

- Concept Talk Video

- Envision It! Animations

- eReaders

Hear It!

- *Sing with Me Animations*

- eSelections

- Grammar Jammer

Adam and Kim play at the beach.

Concept Talk Video

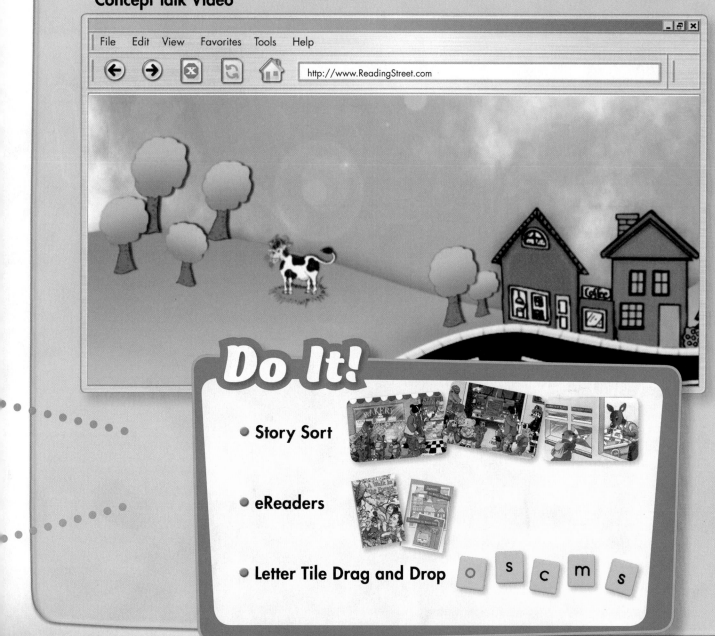

File   Edit   View   Favorites   Tools   Help

http://www.ReadingStreet.com

Do It!

- **Story Sort**

- **eReaders**

- **Letter Tile Drag and Drop**

Changes All Around Us

THE BIG **?** **How do changes affect us?**

Common Core State Standards
Foundational Skills 2. Demonstrate understanding of spoken words, syllables, and sounds (phonemes).
Also Foundational Skills 2.d.

Let's Listen for

Initial Sounds

Read Together

● Point to a nest. Say the word. Say the beginning sound.

■ Point to the baby. Say the word. Say the beginning sound.

▲ Find three pictures that begin with /n/ and three with /b/.

★ Point to these pictures and say the words: *nest, neighbor, fence.* Do they begin the same? What about *bird, baby, bottle?*

♥ Name other words that begin with /n/ and with /b/.

READING STREET ONLINE
BIG QUESTION VIDEO
www.ReadingStreet.com

13

Comprehension

Envision It!

Compare and Contrast

READING STREET ONLINE
ENVISION IT! ANIMATIONS
www.ReadingStreet.com

Envision It! | Sounds to Know

Bb

baby

READING STREET ONLINE
ALPHABET CARDS
www.ReadingStreet.com

Phonics

Initial *Bb*, Initial *Nn*

Words I Can Blend

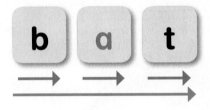

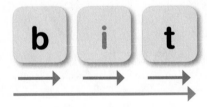

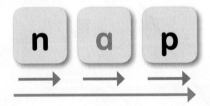

16

Words I Can Read

me

with

she

Sentences I Can Read

1. Nip is with me.
2. She is my cat.
3. Is Nip with Nat?

Common Core State Standards
Foundational Skills 3. Know and apply grade-level phonics and word analysis skills in decoding words.
Also Foundational Skills 3.a., 3.c., 4.

Phonics

I Can Read!

Decodable Reader

- Consonant *Bb*
  bat

■ Consonant *Nn*
  can
  Nat
  Nan

▲ High-Frequency Words
  she
  with
  me

★ Read the story.

READING STREET ONLINE
DECODABLE eREADERS
www.ReadingStreet.com

Nat!

Written by Patricia Crotty
Illustrated by Dan Vick

Decodable Reader 13

Can Nat bat it?
Nat can bat it.

Can Nat tap it?
Nat can tap it.

Can Nat pat it?
Nat can pat it.

Nan can bat it.
She can bat.

Can Nat sip it?
Nat can sip it.

Nat sat with me.

Nat can bat!

Envision It! | Retell

Big Book

Think, Talk, and Write

1. How does a baby panda change as it grows? Text to World

2. How are a baby panda and an adult panda alike? How are they different?

Compare and Contrast

3. Look back and write.

Common Core State Standards
Language 5.a. Sort common objects into categories (e.g., shapes, foods) to gain a sense of the concepts the categories represent. **Also Speaking/Listening 4., 6., Language 6.**

Let's Learn It!

Vocabulary

- What do you see that is black?
- What do you see that is green?
- ▲ What do you see that is brown?

Listening and Speaking

- Act like a character from the story.
- Act like your favorite character from a story.

Color Words

black

green

brown

Respond to Literature
Drama

Be a good speaker!

Let's Practice It!

Poems

- Listen to the two poems.

- Recite each poem. Sway in time to its rhythm.

- Which words rhyme in the first poem? in the second poem?

- How are the two poems alike?

- In the second poem, what does the poet say a star is like?

Star Light, Star Bright

Twinkle, Twinkle, Little Star

Common Core State Standards
Foundational Skills 2.d. Isolate and pronounce the initial, medial vowel, and final sounds (phonemes) in three-phoneme (consonant-vowel-consonant, or CVC) words.

Let's Listen for

Initial Sounds

Read Together

● Point to the red cap. Say *red*. Say the beginning sound.

■ Find three pictures that begin with /r/.

▲ Name other words that begin like *red*.

★ Point to these pictures and say the words: *rose, red, ribbon*. Do they begin the same? What about *nest, baby, bird*?

READING STREET ONLINE
BIG QUESTION VIDEO
www.ReadingStreet.com

Envision It!

Literary Elements

READING STREET ONLINE
ENVISION IT! ANIMATIONS
www.ReadingStreet.com

Characters

Setting

Plot

Common Core State Standards
Foundational Skills 3.a. Demonstrate basic knowledge of one-to-one letter-sound correspondences by producing the primary or many of the most frequent sounds for each consonant.
Also Foundational Skills 2.d., 3.c.

Envision It! | Sounds to Know

Rr

river

READING STREET ONLINE
ALPHABET CARDS
www.ReadingStreet.com

Phonics

🎯 Initial *Rr*

Words I Can Blend

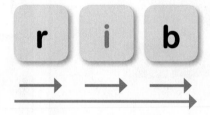

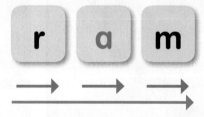

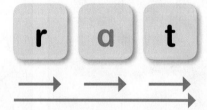

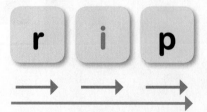

Words I Can Read

me

with

she

Sentences I Can Read

1. Nan ran with me.

2. She ran to my cat.

3. We ran with Ric.

Common Core State Standards
Foundational Skills 4. Read emergent-reader texts with purpose and understanding.
Also Foundational Skills 3.a., 3.c.

Phonics

I Can Read!

Decodable Reader

- ● Consonant *Rr*
  Rip
  rat
  ran
  Rap

- ■ High-Frequency Words
  the
  a
  she
  with
  me

- ▲ Read the story.

READING STREET ONLINE
DECODABLE eREADERS
www.ReadingStreet.com

Rip with Rap

Written by Peggy Lee
Illustrated by Lucy Smythe

Decodable Reader 14

Rip the rat can sit.

Rip sat in a cap.
Rip sat.

Rip ran in the can.
Rip ran.

Rip sat in the can.
Rip sat.

Rip can bat the cap.
She can bat it.

Rip is with me.
Rip can sit.

Rip can nap.
Rap can bat.

Common Core State Standards
Literature 1. With prompting and support, ask and answer questions about key details in a text. **Also Literature 2.**

Envision It! Retell

Trade Book

Think, Talk, and Write

1. What new things have you learned to do? **Text to Self**

2.

Beginning	
Middle	
End	

Choose an important part of the story. Act it out with some friends.  Plot

3. Look back and write.

Let's Learn It!

Vocabulary

- Talk about the pictures.
- Name actions you do.

Listening and Speaking

- Show how to do something.
- Tell how you do it.
- ▲ Speak in complete sentences.

Action Words

walk

run

fly

swim

Sequence

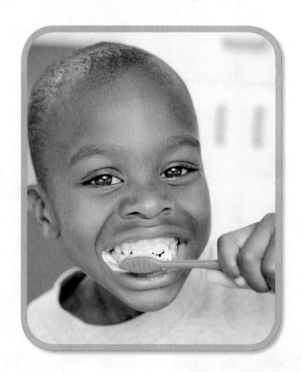

Be a good speaker!

49

Common Core State Standards
Literature 3. With prompting and support, identify characters, setting, and major events in a story. **Also Literature 1., 5.**

Rumpelstiltskin

Let's Practice It!

Fairy Tale

● Listen to the fairy tale.

■ What do the words *Once upon a time* tell you about the story?

▲ When and where does the story take place?

★ Describe the character Rumpelstiltskin.

♥ What happens in threes in the story?

Common Core State Standards
Foundational Skills 2. Demonstrate understanding of spoken words, syllables, and sounds (phonemes).

Phonemic Awareness

Let's Listen for

Initial Sounds

Read Together

● Point to a deer. Say the word. Say the beginning sound.

■ Point to *kick*. Say the word. Say the beginning sound.

▲ Find three pictures that begin with /d/ and /k/.

★ Name other words that begin with /d/ and /k/.

**READING STREET ONLINE
BIG QUESTION VIDEO**
www.ReadingStreet.com

52

53

Common Core State Standards
Informational Text 3. With prompting and support, describe the connection between two individuals, events, ideas, or pieces of information in a text.

Envision It!

Cause and Effect

Common Core State Standards
Foundational Skills 2.d. Isolate and pronounce the initial, medial vowel, and final sounds (phonemes) in three-phoneme (consonant-vowel-consonant, or CVC) words.
Also Foundational Skills 3.a., 3.c.

Envision It! | **Sounds to Know**

Kk

koala

READING STREET ONLINE
ALPHABET CARDS
www.ReadingStreet.com

Phonics

Initial *Kk*, Initial *Dd*

Words I Can Blend

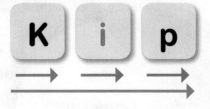

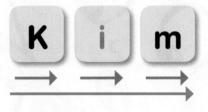

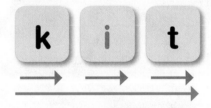

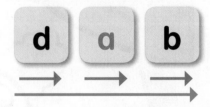

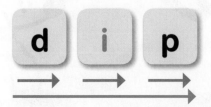

Words I Can Read

see

look

Sentences I Can Read

1. I see Kip.

2. We can look at Kim.

3. Look. Can we see Kip?

Common Core State Standards
Foundational Skills 4. Read emergent-reader texts with purpose and understanding.
Also Literature 2.,
Foundational Skills 3.a., 3.c.

Phonics

I Can Read!

Decodable Reader

- Consonant *Dd*
  did
  Dad
  kid

- Consonant *Kk*
  kid

- High-Frequency Words
  see
  the
  look

★ Read the story.

♥ After reading, retell the story.

READING STREET ONLINE
DECODABLE eREADERS
www.ReadingStreet.com

Dad Did

Written by June Harper
Illustrated by Bethany Mills

Did Dad see the cat?
Dad did.

Did Dad look at it?
Dad did.

Did Dad see the rat?
Dad did.

Did Dad look at it?
Dad did.

Did Dad see the kid?
Dad did.

Did Dad look at it?
Dad did.

Dad can.
Dad did.

Common Core State Standards
Literature 1. With prompting and support, ask and answer questions about key details in a text. **Also Literature 2.**

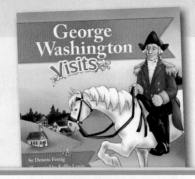

George Washington Visits

by Dennis Fertig

Big Book

Envision It! | Retell

1

2

3

4

5

6

Think, Talk, and Write

1. How is this town's celebration like the one in *We Are So Proud?* Text to Text

2. What did Daniel and Father do in the story? Why did they do it? Cause and Effect

3. Look back and write.

Common Core State Standards
Foundational Skills 2.a. Recognize and produce rhyming words. **Also Language 6.**

Let's Learn It!

Vocabulary

- ● Talk about the pictures.
- ■ Put your hand over your head.
- ▲ Put your finger under your nose.
- ★ Put your hand on your knee.
- ♥ Sit in a circle around your teacher.

Listening and Speaking

- ● Name words that rhyme with *man*, *black*, and *cat*.
- ■ Say a rhyme.
- ▲ Make up a rhyme of your own.

Position Words

over

under

on

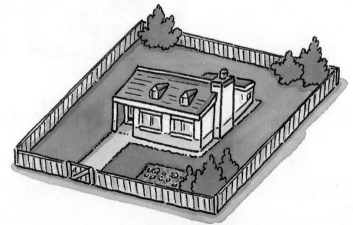

around

68

Recite Rhymes

Be a good speaker!

Get Ready For Grade 1

69

Can Celery Sip?

Step 1

Let's Practice It!

Science Experiment

- Listen to the science experiment.

- What is this experiment about?

- In which step do you use the scissors?

- What makes the celery change color?

- What questions do you have about the experiment?

Step 2

Step 3

Step 4

Step 5

71

Common Core State Standards
Foundational Skills 2. Demonstrate understanding of spoken words, syllables, and sounds (phonemes). **Also Foundational Skills 2.a.**

Let's Listen for

Initial Sounds

Read Together

- ● Point to the fence. Say the word. Say the beginning sound.

- ■ Find three things that begin with /f/, like *fence*.

- ▲ Say these words: *feet, food, dress.* Do they begin with the same sound? What about *first, finger, fast*?

- ★ What rhymes with *fish*?

READING STREET ONLINE
BIG QUESTION VIDEO
www.ReadingStreet.com

72

Comprehension

Envision It!

Literary Elements

READING STREET ONLINE
ENVISION IT! ANIMATIONS
www.ReadingStreet.com

Characters

Setting

Plot

Common Core State Standards
Foundational Skills 3.a. Demonstrate basic knowledge of one-to-one letter-sound correspondences by producing the primary or many of the most frequent sounds for each consonant.
Also Foundational Skills 2.d., 3.c.

Envision It! | **Sounds to Know**

Ff

fountain

READING STREET ONLINE
ALPHABET CARDS
www.ReadingStreet.com

Phonics

Initial *Ff*

Words I Can Blend

Words I Can Read

see

look

Sentences I Can Read

1. We look for a fin.
2. I see a fin!
3. Look at it.

Common Core State Standards
Foundational Skills 4. Read emergent-reader texts with purpose and understanding.
Also Foundational Skills 1.a., 3.a., 3.c.

Phonics

I Can Read!

Decodable Reader

- Consonant *Ff*
  fan
  fat
  fit

- High-Frequency Words
  see
  a
  look
  the

▲ Read the story.

READING STREET ONLINE
DECODABLE eREADERS
www.ReadingStreet.com

In the Kit!

Written by Leon Cross
Illustrated by Jeff Blake

Decodable Reader 16

Kip can see a kit.

Kip can look in it.

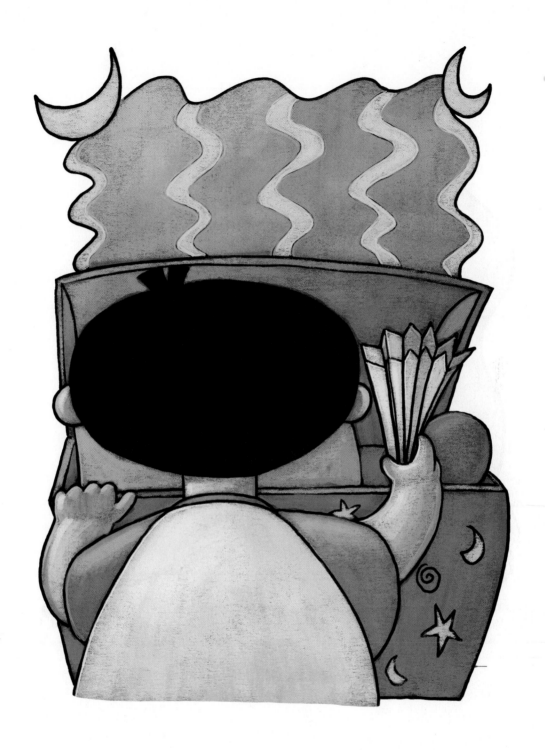

Kip can see a fan.

Kip can fan.
Fan, Kip, fan.

Kip can see a fat cat.

Kip can pat.
Pat, Kip, pat.

Kip can fit it in the kit.

Common Core State Standards

Literature 1. With prompting and support, ask and answer questions about key details in a text. **Also Literature 2.**

Tradebook

Envision It! | Retell

READING STREET ONLINE
STORY SORT
www.ReadingStreet.com

86

Think, Talk, and Write

1. Which grows like you? <small>**Text to Self**</small>

2.

Beginning	
Middle	
End	

Choose an important part of the story. Act it out with some friends. ↻ **Plot**

3. Look back and write.

Let's Learn It!

Vocabulary

- Talk about the pictures.
- Show you are happy.
- When might you feel sad?
- Show you are excited.
- When might you be surprised?

Listening and Speaking

- Tell a story about how you've grown.

Vocabulary

Words for Feelings

happy

sad

excited

surprised

Oral Presentation

Be a good speaker!

Common Core State Standards
Literature 1. With prompting and support, ask and answer questions about key details in a text. **Also Literature 5.**

Let's Practice It! ①

Fable

● Listen to the fable.

■ What problem do the mice have?

▲ What is the young mouse's idea?

★ What does the old mouse say about this idea?

♥ How can the fable's moral help you with your ideas?

The Mice and The Cat

91

Common Core State Standards

Foundational Skills 2. Demonstrate understanding of spoken words, syllables, and sounds (phonemes).

Phonemic Awareness

Let's Listen for

Initial Sounds

Read Together

● Say *Oscar*. What sound do you hear at the beginning of *Oscar*?

■ Find three pictures that begin with /o/.

▲ Name other words that begin with /o/.

★ Say these words: *Oscar, Otto, oxen*. Do they begin the same? What about *April, olive, onion*?

**READING STREET ONLINE
BIG QUESTION VIDEO**
www.ReadingStreet.com

BOOK SALE

Envision It!

Draw Conclusions

READING STREET ONLINE
ENVISION IT! ANIMATIONS
www.ReadingStreet.com

Happy Happy Happy

Common Core State Standards
Foundational Skills 3. Know and apply grade-level phonics and word analysis skills in decoding words.
Also Foundational Skills 2.d., 3.a., 3.b., 3.c.

Envision It! Sounds to Know

Oo

otter

READING STREET ONLINE
ALPHABET CARDS
www.ReadingStreet.com

Short o

Words I Can Blend

R o n

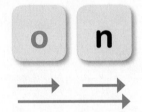

o n

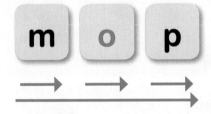

m o p

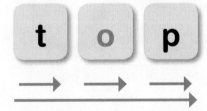

t o p

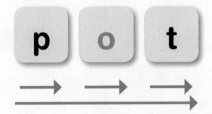

p o t

96

Words I Can Read

they

you

of

Sentences I Can Read

1. Can you see me?
2. They can see me.
3. I am on top of Dad.

Common Core State Standards
Foundational Skills 3. Know and apply grade-level phonics and word analysis skills in decoding words.
Also Foundational Skills 3.a., 3.c., 4.

Phonics

I Can Read!

Decodable Reader

● Short *o*
Tom
mop
on
top
cot
Dot

■ High-Frequency Words
of
the
they
look
you

▲ Read the story.

Decodable Reader 17

The Mop

Written by Donald Newman
Illustrated by Marcia Geller

Can Tom mop?
Tom can mop.

Tom can nap on
top of the cot.

Can Dot mop?
Dot can mop.

Dot can sit on
top of the cot.

Can Pat mop?
Pat can mop.

Pat can fit on
top of the cot.

They look at the mop.
Can you mop?

Envision It! Retell

Big Book

Written by Tracy Sato
Illustrated by Ute Simon

1

2

3

4

5

6

READING STREET ONLINE
STORY SORT
www.ReadingStreet.com

Think, Talk, and Write

1. How have games changed over the years? *Text to World*

2. How would our lives be different if we still used these things? *Draw Conclusions*

3. Look back and write.

Let's Learn It!

Vocabulary

- Talk about the pictures.
- ■ Look around for things that are new and old.
- ▲ Tell about something that is fast.
- ★ Tell about something that is slow.

Listening and Speaking

- Tell a message to a partner.
- ■ Listen to your partner's message.
- ▲ Retell the message.

Vocabulary

Words for Opposites

new

old

fast

slow

Messages

Be a good speaker!

109

Common Core State Standards
Literature 1. With prompting and support, ask and answer questions about key details in a text. **Also Literature 2.**

How Coyote Helped People

①

Let's
Practice
It!

Folk Tale

- Listen to the folk tale.

- What two things does the folk tale explain?

- ▲ What can you learn from the way Coyote behaves?

- ⭐ Coyote appears in many Native American folk tales. Why do you think this is so?

Let's Listen for

Initial Sounds

Read Together

- ● Say the sound you hear at the beginning of *octopus, bed, nest, red, desk, car, fun.*

- ■ Point to the octopus. Find another picture that begins like *octopus.*

- ▲ Now find pictures that begin with /b/, /n/, /r/, /d/, /k/, /f/.

- ★ Say *octopus, otter, ox.* What sound do you hear at the beginning of these words?

READING STREET ONLINE
BIG QUESTION VIDEO
www.ReadingStreet.com

113

Comprehension

Envision It!

Main Idea

READING STREET ONLINE
ENVISION IT! ANIMATIONS
www.ReadingStreet.com

School

Envision It! | **Sounds to Know**

Oo

otter

**READING STREET ONLINE
ALPHABET CARDS**
www.ReadingStreet.com

Phonics

Short o

Words I Can Blend

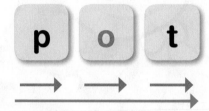

p o t

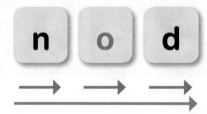

p o d

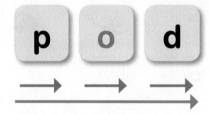

n o d

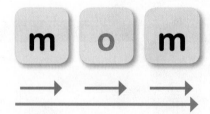

m o m

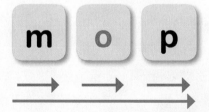

m o p

Words I Can Read

they

you

of

Sentences I Can Read

1. They like you.

2. They can see Mom.

3. Sit on top of Mom.

Common Core State Standards
Foundational Skills 3. Know and apply grade-level phonics and word analysis skills in decoding words.
Also Foundational Skills 3.b., 3.c., 4.

Phonics

I Can Read!

Decodable Reader

● Short *o*
Rod
top
Don
not
on
cot
Dot

■ High-Frequency Words
the
you
is
of
they

▲ Read the story.

♥ After reading, retell the story.

READING STREET ONLINE
DECODABLE eREADERS
www.ReadingStreet.com

Tip the Top

Written by Page Kuhl

Illustrated by David Muntz

Decodable Reader 18

Rod can pat it.
Rod can tip the top.

Don can pat it.
Don did tip it.

You did not tip the top.

It is on top of the cot.

Dot did not tip it.

They can pat the top.
They can tip it.

It can not tip!

Common Core State Standards
Literature 2. With prompting and support, retell familiar stories, including key details.
Also Literature 1.

Trade Book

Envision It! | Retell

Think, Talk, and Write

1. How does the mouse help the lion? Text to World

2. What lesson did you learn from this story?

Main Idea

3. Look back and write.

Common Core State Standards
Speaking/Listening 3. Ask and answer questions in order to seek help, get information, or clarify something that is not understood. **Also Language 5.c., 6.**

Let's Learn It!

Vocabulary

- Talk about the pictures.

■ Look around. Name things that are hard. Name things that are soft.

▲ Name things that are smooth.

★ Name things that are rough.

Listening and Speaking

- Ask classmates a question about a picture.

■ Answer a classmate's question with a complete sentence.

Words for Textures

hard

soft

rough

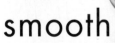

smooth

Ask and Answer Questions

Be a good listener!

Lions

Common Core State Standards
Informational Text 1. With prompting and support, ask and answer questions about key details in a text.
Also Informational Text 2.

Let's Practice It! ①

Expository Text

● Look at the title and the pictures. What will the selection be about?

■ Listen to the selection.

▲ How do lions get their food?

★ What do lions have that helps them hunt?

♥ Why do people read selections like this one?

Words for Things That Go

airplane

bike

truck

car

bus

van

boat

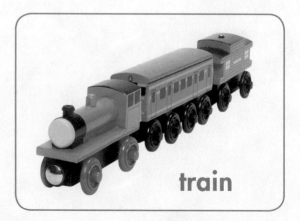

train

Words for Colors

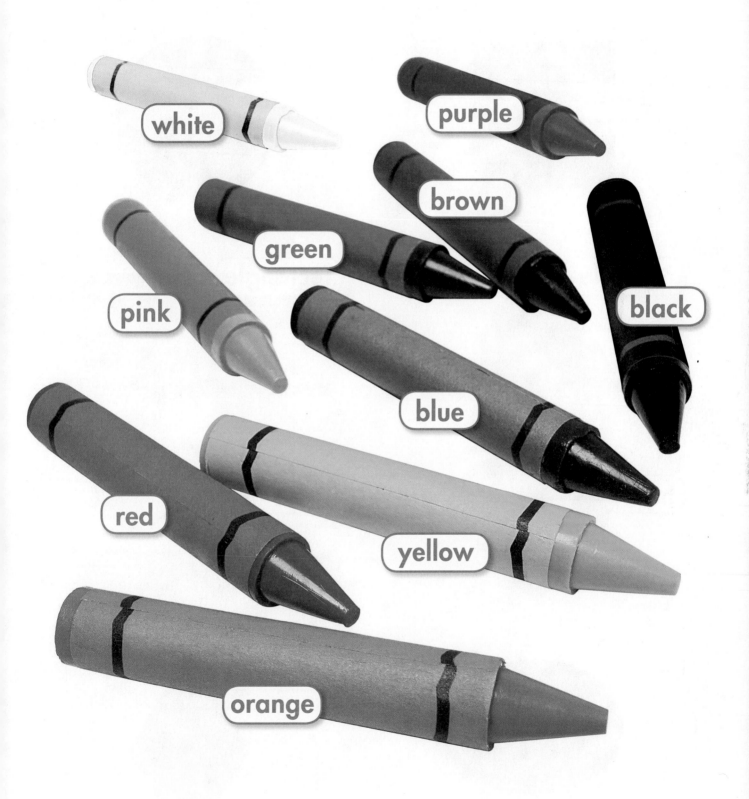

white

purple

brown

green

black

pink

blue

red

yellow

orange

Words for Shapes

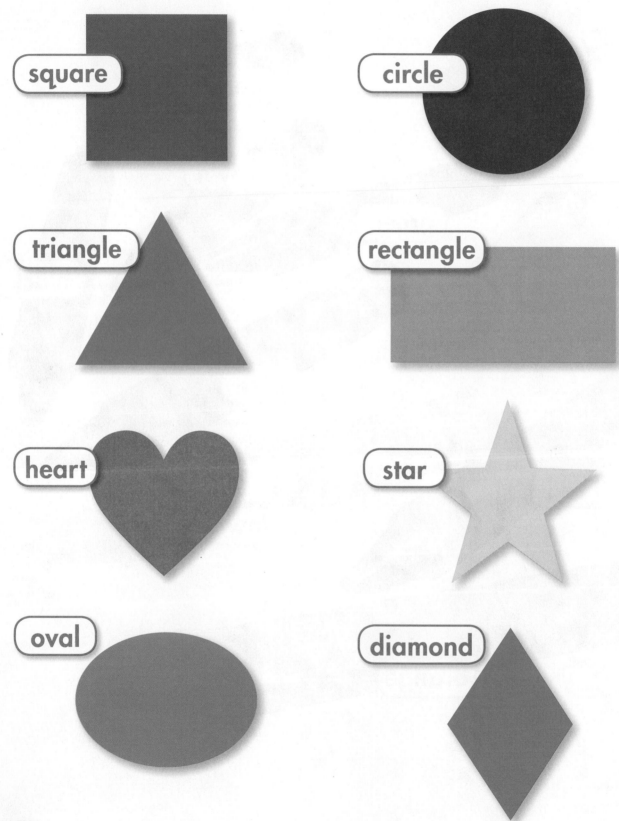

square

circle

triangle

rectangle

heart

star

oval

diamond

Words for Places

school

home

park

train station

police station

fire station

post office

library

Words for Animals

lion

mouse

puppy

dog

cat

duck

turtle

kitten

chick

hen

rooster

bird

fish

whale

butterfly

caterpillar

bear

panda

beaver

calf

cow

Words for Actions

skip

walk

run

fly

swim

ride

jump

hop

Position Words

up

in

out

down

on

around

over

under

My Classroom

bookcase

easel

books

desk

markers

crayons

pencils

teacher

toys

paper

chair

blocks

table

rug

Words for Feelings

happy

frightened

worried

excited

angry

proud

sad

surprised

My Family

mom
mother

dad
father

sister

grandmother

grandfather

brother

Acknowledgments

Illustrations

Cover: Rob Hefferan

12 Mary Sullivan

28, 68, 88, 108–109 Mick Reid

30 Ken Wilson Max

32 Kellie Lewis

39–45 Natalia Vasquez

50–51 Daniel Griffo

52 Miki Sakamoto

59–65, 119–125 Maria Mola

72 Stacy Curtis

79–85 Dani Jones

90–91 Aaron Zenz

92 Suwin Chan

99–105 Wednesday Kirwan

110–111 Linda Bronson

112 Akemi Gutierrez

Photographs

Every effort has been made to secure permission and provide appropriate credit for photographic material. The publisher deeply regrets any omission and pledges to correct errors called to its attention in subsequent editions.

Unless otherwise acknowledged, all photographs are the property of Pearson Education, Inc.

Photo locators denoted as follows: Top (T), Center (C), Bottom (B), Left (L), Right (R), Background (Bkgd)

10 (B) ©Steve Bloom Images/Jupiter Images

36 ©E.G. Hellier/Robert Harding Picture Library, Ltd.

48 ©Chuck Franklin/Alamy Images, ©Hal Beral/Corbis, ©Mika/zefa/Corbis, Jupiter Images

49 ©Bill Frymire/Masterfile Corporation, ©Michael Newman/PhotoEdit, Inc., BananaStock

56 ©Gerard Lacz/Animals Animals/Earth Scenes

69 ©Buzz Pictures/Alamy, ©D. Hurst/Alamy, ©DK Images, Frank Greenaway/©DK Images, Peter Chadwick/©DK Images, Tim Ridley/©DK Images

76 ©Nik Wheeler/Corbis

87 (B) ©Arthur Morris/Corbis; (C) ©Lynda Richardson/Corbis

89 ©Phil Savoie/Nature Picture Library, ©Philippe Clement/Nature Picture Library

96 Dave King/DK Images

116 Dave King/DK Images

128 ©Visuals Unlimited/Corbis, Corbis, Mike Dunning/©DK Images

130 (B) ©Roderick Edwards/Animals Animals/Earth Scenes

131 (T) ©ABPL/Clem Haagner/Animals Animals/Earth Scenes, (B) ©Michael Fogden/Animals Animals/Earth Scenes, (C) ©Peter Weimann/Animals Animals/Earth Scenes

132 (CR) ©Basement Stock/Alamy, (TR, TL, TC, BL) Getty Images

133 (B) Getty Images

135 (BCL) ©Guillen Photography/Alamy Images, (BCR) ©Kinn Deacon/Alamy Images, (BR) Flavio Beltran/Shutterstock, (TCR) Photos to Go/Photolibrary

136 (BR) ©Arthur Morris/Corbis, (CC) ©Cyril Laubscher/DK Images, (TL) ©Dave King/DK Images, (BC) ©Gordon Clayton/DK Images, (CR) ©Karl Shone/DK Images, (CL) ©Marc Henrie/DK Images, (TR) DK Images, (TC, BCL) Getty Images, (BL) Jane Burton/(c)DK Images

137 (CR) ©A. Ramey/PhotoEdit, ©Comstock Images/Jupiter Images, (CL) ©Cyndy Black/Robert Harding World Imagery, (CC) ©Dave King/DK Images, (BR, BC) ©Gordon Clayton/DK Images, ©Rudi Von Briel/PhotoEdit, (TC, BL) Getty Images

138 (TR) ©Rubberball Productions, (BR) Jupiter Images, (TL) Photodisc/Thinkstock/Getty Images, (BC) Photos to Go/Photolibrary, (TC) Steve Shott/©DK Images

139 (TR, TC) ©Max Oppenheim/Getty Images, (CR, BR) Getty Images, (C, BL) Rubberball Productions

142 (CR) ©Ellen B. Senisi, (BL) ©Simon Marcus/Corbis, (TR, TL) Getty Images, (TC) Jupiter Images, (C) Photos to Go/Photolibrary, (BR) Rubberball Productions